Memoirs 1910 to 1936 That Shaped My Life

3-15-05

Memoirs 1910 to 1936 That Shaped My Life

Joseph Louis Klein

Deputy Chief Inspector (Retired),
NYPD

VANTAGE PRESS
New York

Cover design by Susan Thomas

FIRST EDITION

Published by Vantage Press, Inc.
419 Park Ave. South, New York, NY 10016

Manufactured in the United States of America
ISBN: 0-533-14762-X

Library of Congress Catalog Card No.: 2003097059

0 9 8 7 6 5 4 3 2 1

To my sisters, my pals,
who in my youthful years
were my charges and my responsibilities

Contents

Preface

These memoirs of events that shaped my life are the preludes that triggered the author to write: *THE POLICE CAREER: An Endless Challenge* a paperback introduced to the literary market in December 1996, published by Vantage Press, Inc.

While these memoirs in no way relate to or smack of anything of a police nature, they cover a period of time from 1910, the time of my blessed event, to 1936.

These memoirs are so varied, unique, and interesting, that they are beyond challenge and comparison; in a class by themselves.

Passing through the various stages of life, we are motivated and obsessed by fantasies, dreams, and ambitions hopefully to reach a satisfying goal in life. To realize each in turn, each must be pursued to the point of success or failure. While these litmus-test operations are in progress, an evaluation process must be in vogue to foresee what potentials exist for a future goal in life. There is no opportunity for discouragement. Self-discipline and hard work are necessary elements to inspire us.

The trial-and-error periods of our life should finely hone our talents to be able to make a decision that leads to a successful goal in life.

Thus in March 1936, I took my oath of office as a member of The New York City Police Department initiating what culminated in a thirty-five-year career. The net results of my memoirs: I played Broadway and I patrolled Broadway.

Memoirs
1910 to 1936
That Shaped My Life

1

Manhattan, East Village, 1910

I have no personal knowledge of this, but through the years my parents told me that my blessed event took place on July 20, 1910. The location was a six-story tenement on Sixth Street between Avenues A and B on the East Side of Manhattan, an area now known as the East Village. I also learned that I had a brother named Otto, after my dad, who possibly was standing by anticipating precious moments with me in the later years.

Maternity deliveries at that time took place at home with the family doctor and a midwife in attendance.

It was a red-letter day for my parents, and for me to say that I was aware of what was happening would be fallacious. From life's experience, I know that my derriere was slapped to see if I qualified for alto, bass, or soprano. I can imagine that with squinty eyes and drooling, I surveyed my surroundings, working my arms and legs wildly asserting myself and introducing myself to my new world. I was baptized, Joseph Louis.

I have little remembrance of my brother Otto, except for a picture, still in my possession, taken of both of us, cooling off, enjoying gentle summer breezes sitting on the fire escape, the luxury piazza of a tenement.

I have no recollection of my brother's death, but it

The sixth-floor fire escape of my tenement residence. Brother Otto on right, author on left. A brotherly relationship, short-lived—a picture of innocence personified, oblivious to worldly challenges.

must have happened during my early years, when serious happenings leave no lasting impressions.

My mom's name was Elizabeth Wilhemina, and Dad responded to Otto Emerick. My dad at this time was employed by the City of New York as a fireman, operating out of Engine Company #28 located at 222 East 2nd Street. At one time when a fire occurred in a loft building on Avenue B, I remember seeing my dad working at a top-story window. Fire engines during these years were not motorized. They were horse-drawn. What a picture that would make today, to see horses racing to the scene of a fire. A picture to remember if this took place today.

In retrospect my youthful years were rough and tumble. The tenement that I lived in was a six-story job. The higher you lived, the cheaper the rent. They were called cold-water flats, with a coal stove for cooking, baking, and general family needs. The commode was shared with your neighbor. Building codes did not require elevators for six stories and above. That apparently was considered too luxurious and not affordable.

The ground floor at street level was occupied by two stores. On entering the building, on the right was an undertaker's parlor named Erlick. On the left was a barber shop with the usual red-and-white pole on the sidewalk to mark its location.

A long narrow hall, ill kept with garbage cans, sometimes baby carriages, led to the yard. How well I remember this, for there was a trellis that supported a grape vine that on occasion bore fruit. It appeared that the vine when in bloom was a haven for caterpillars, a species of which I have never seen since. They were a rainbow of colors, not fuzzy, probably extinct at this time. An old-fashioned pump with a long handle, still operative, stood majestically in one corner.

I was baptized at the Most Holy Redeemer R.C. Church on 3rd Street. Horse-drawn trolley cars were the mode of travel from the East to the West side of Manhattan along Third Street.

I remember attending services at this church. On special occasions, when processions were to take place as part of the ceremony, a men's society known as the Hessian Guards, in full regalia, including swords and plummed hats, would in military formation march with the other church sodalities. I might add that this was a German neighborhood at this time.

When something of a horrendous nature took place, a hawkster would work the neighborhood, shouting, "Extra! Extra! Read all about it." I remember well that this happened when a policeman was shot and killed in an alley on the church grounds.

I know very little of both my mother's or father's background. My dad's father was named Nitus. He was a cobbler from the old country, I assume Austria, since at one time in later years, I received a pocket watch from him that bore a black cross on its rear. I understand that he received this watch from a Franz Joseph, in his homeland.

My dad's mother was named Anna. The family lived on Rivington Street between Willet and Sheriff Streets in Manhattan. My dad was the oldest of five children, Anna, Louis, Emil, and Frank.

My dad often spoke of how at age twelve he was doing a man's job to help in support of his family. As a result my dad had no childhood, which labeled him through life as a man of all work and no play.

I know very little of my mom's background, except that there were two aunts, Julia and Margaret, along with Grandpa John Schoepf, who lived in New Jersey. Incidentally, my mother's maiden name was Jahrsdoepher, a died-in-the-wool name from German ancestry.

In retrospect, my youthful years were rough and tumble. There were not too many places for children to play. There was a beautiful park, Tompkins Square, a block distant, but that was off limits for me alone.

When I was permitted on the street alone, close to home, I had to be within calling distance of my mom, who would shout from a window on the top floor of a six-story tenement.

There were youngsters in the area, my age bracket, and we were considered playmates. Sometimes differences took over and altercations resulted. The reasons seemed important at the time, but of no substance now, when viewing them as an adult.

In one incident, I was struck on the head with a two-by-two post. On another occasion, I had a fight for honor. Chasing my opponent into his father's glazier shop, I, just upon entering the store, was struck behind my left ear by a putty knife that was thrown by my assailant as I ducked. The appearance of blood ended the fight. I ran home and found my mom hanging wash on the roof washline. My mom, acting quickly, sought medical attention, and the culprit was disciplined by his parents. I realize now that my mom at this time was with child, a sister to be named Marie.

The neighborhood had its share of cafés, so different from our pubs today. They appeared to be family places for dining and fun. During the hot summer months, long before air conditioning, doors would be left open, and Gypsy violin music would permeate the area.

While each man's home is and was his castle, it was not too comfortable living in a tenement with windows wide open to catch the breezes. The roof was the refuge spot for this luxury. Then, too, many a night was spent sleeping on a fire escape for the same purpose. During daylight hours, one could scan surrounding rooftop areas and see neighbors in similar situations.

Flying kites from rooftops, at this time, was a hobby and recreation enjoyed by all ages. They were inexpensive toys and when caught in a gust of wind would float like a soap balloon to great heights, depending on the size of the ball of twine in the hands of the operator. Some kites had long rag tails while others were triangular shaped, all inexpensive toys. When a kite was flying at some three hundred feet, it was interesting to note the force of the air currents on the twine in your hand.

Horse-drawn vehicles were the mode of business and making deliveries during this period. Naturally, the streets had to be kept clean so the City Sanitation Department employed street cleaners all dressed in white. Each in turn had his own cart that he pushed, plus all necessary equipment to perform well.

As the years rolled by, the street cleaners were referred to as "sanitation engineers" to lend dignity. We all know that today, we use highly sophisticated sweepers that do the work more efficiently and quickly.

A hobby that we seldom see today, yet may still exist in ghetto quarters, is flying pigeons from rooftops. Years ago, I assume that building maintenance codes were not as we have them today. Pigeon coops were erected on rooftops. The pigeon fanciers, referred to as "Pigeon Mikes," would stock their coops with thirty or more pigeons as a flock.

After the pigeons were cooped, fed, and adjusted themselves to their new home, the owners would fly them for exercise and show. A street away, another "Pigeon Mike" would set up his operation in similar style and fly them when it was reasonably certain that they would return. The "Pigeon Mikes" would usually fly their flocks at the same time, with the hope of enticing one or two of the other flock to join theirs. These men apparently knew all of their birds and would immediately recognize a situation such as this, if his flock increased or decreased by one or two birds. Many families complained, for in some instances, their freshly washed clothes drying on lines were soiled.

I imagine that through the years all of this has been changed by updating building codes, for this all took place circa 1915.

It was nothing uncommon, for in early years, pretzel vendors were many. They usually carried a huge basket studded with sticks displaying a variety of pretzels.

On one occasion a vendor, who must have followed me, cornered me in the hallway of my building at the doorway leading to the cellar. As I remember, he was a disheveled and disgusting individual with a leering look in his eyes. Pretzels were hanging from his basket. I realized that he was a bad man. As he cornered me real close to the cellar door, he leaned over and said, "Tell me that you love me." I must have been four or five years old at that time, but nonetheless quick thinking, for I scooted under his basket and ran up five flights to my mother. She was startled when she heard my story and shouted, alerting the neighbors. A local search was made without results.

My mom always kept me neat and trim. As I remember, I was all in white, wearing knickers. Don't ask me why or where I found it, but a small box of matches caught my eye and being fascinated, I found a place for them in my right pants pocket. My mom, with eagle-eye, noticed the bulge in my white pants pocket and asked what I had there. I am not going to elaborate on what took place, but I paid the penalty to my mom and when my dad came home.

My mom had a school chum, Minnie Nack, who resided in Carnarsie, stop by for a visit with her daughter Rose who was approximately my age. Rose and I were having a grand time swinging around, and before I could realize it, I was hugging the freshly painted barber pole. At the time, I was wearing a chinchilla coat. Our laughter almost turned to tears when we realized what had happened. My nice coat now bore the design of the freshly painted barber pole. Even at five years, I was completely embarrassed in view of my friend's knowing how I would be punished later by my parents. It all remains vivid in my mind as though it only happened yesterday.

One day about noon, a parade took place going north along Avenue A, in the vicinity of Seventh Street Park, Tompkins Square. I have no idea as to what prompted this parade nor what was being celebrated. A segment of it was a display of fire engines, all horse-drawn, with my dad participating, holding on to the rear of Engine Company 28. The occasion drew many sidewalk spectators. Seeing my dad made me feel rather proud. Lo and behold, my mom gave a fast jerk and I wondered what happened. Some wise guy in the crowd had given my mom a pat on her rear. She was startled, and the man took off. Apparently my dad, who had his eye on us in passing, realized something had happened. He left his position in the parade, but before he learned what had happened, the culprit responsible had taken off and was lost in the crowd. I must have been in the five-year age bracket, because I remember this well.

Both Mom and Dad started to tell me how they were planning to move to a new home in Queens. I asked a natural question: why? Their answer was that it was a nicer place to live. It was cleaner, with better homes and studded with trees. I listened intently and my next remembrance was that we were living on Catalpa Avenue in Queens.

2
Queens, 1915

Our stay was brief at this location and now we were living in a two-family house at 2405 Hughes Street. The people who owned this house—their name was Hellman, a German family with their three daughters. I can't tell you why, but I remember one's name was Erika. The father was a glass blower. His workshop was his basement where many a time I watched him make Christmas balls and various ornaments, blowing long tubes of glass heated over a Bunsen burner.

I was approaching school age when my mom and dad moved to 1857 Putnam Avenue, a development known as Mathew's Flats, between Onderdonk and Forest Avenues. There again we lived on the top floor, a walk-up, because the rent was cheaper. As a youngster, I could see the improvement by comparing where we lived in Manhattan. Most importantly we had our own bathroom, and the surroundings were all neat and clean. It was there where my mom gave birth to my sister Marie.

Our doctor's name was Kemp, and the midwife who assisted lived a few houses away. Her name was Mrs. Dorn. I was so happy to have a sister. She at this time was going through the same phase of life that I went through, when the doctor slapped my butt. I don't remember too much of my sister Marie, but I assume we were very close, for she died in my arms, as I watched her eyes roll during a convulsion spell. Details after this happening are rather fuzzy on my part, for I have no recollection of her having any ailment. Being young, I found this period of sadness was short-lived in my memory.

I was enrolled in the parochial school at St. Mathias Parish on Catalpa Avenue, some three streets from my home. The school was run by Notre Dame nuns from grade one to and including the eighth grade. As I remember there were some thirty nuns with a Mother Superior named Sister Alcantara in charge. The habit that they wore was all black, with a heavily starched white head piece that picture-framed their faces.

My school days and educational career had now been started. The day began by attending eight A.M. Mass, then an assembly in the school yard, and off to the assigned classroom where an assigned nun took over for the full day. Twelve noon, with the sounding of the Angelus bells, meant lunchtime, off to home, returning at one P.M. I can't remember anything unusual during my early years, except for being away from home with other children. All of the classes were co-ed. Yes, there was homework and my parents displayed their talents in helping me. During class we had our moments of fun and laughter, but when someone became a little misbehaved, he or she had to sit with their hands either on their head or behind their back for a certain period of time.

At age eight, I found myself in the third grade with a different nun as teacher. All of the original class passed "en masse," which made it nice, for after a period of two years we got to know each other.

On June 18, 1918, my parents presented me with a new member of the family, my sister Agnes. Aside from my parents helping me progress at school, there was a newcomer in the family to take care of.

As I remember there were three priests assigned to the parish. Father Wagner who had two police dogs as pets was pastor, Fathers Ranker and Hoffmen were his co-workers.

Now being in the third grade at age eight, I enrolled as an altar boy. This was a challenge, for weekly meetings were held by Father Ranker. Instructions were given, and it was necessary at that time to learn the Latin Mass prayers.

There must have been some forty altar boys who assembled each week for instructions in the school assembly hall. Yes, each one was tested and had to recite certain prayers in Latin. Learning and saying these prayers were a must, for they were said at Mass at times with the priest. Then, too, there were bells that were sounded at certain times during the Mass. Some of the older boys, seventh and eighth graders, at times were a little cocky to the newer members.

When serving any Mass, four altar boys were usually in attendance to help celebrate and assist the priest. There were four positions for the boys at Mass: high right, high left, low right and low left. The older boys would usually take over the positions of high right and high left. These two would assist the priest with the cruets, holding the wine and water. The low right position was responsible for ringing the bells, while the low left just knelt on the marble step, a sort of penance, and had no responsibility except to be present. When the priest distributed Communion, the high right server held the gold plate under each communicant's chin while the priest advanced along the altar rail.

For years, I served daily at the six thirty A.M. Mass. It

was interesting and spiritually inspiring, especially during Christmas and the Holy Week prior to Easter, when altar boys were always gracing the tabernacle on kneelers in prayer for two-hour periods.

The conduct among some forty altar boys was not always what it should have been. None of us wore halos. Sometimes the older boys would tie knots in our cassock sleeves just to assert themselves. I personally remember engaging in a fist fight in the school alley after Mass with one of my associates.

Each summer the priests, in appreciation for our dedication to duties, would plan an outing for the forty altar boys in the Rockaways at a beach resort for a day of swimming, with a delicious seafood dinner to climax the day.

It being a German parish, an idea was conceived to have a German study program, on Saturdays in the convent. The program included writing the German hieroglyphics. It was a voluntary program, and my parents had me enrolled. I remember attending on several Saturdays, but when World War I was declared on April 6, 1917, that put the damper on this program. Rumor spread throughout the neighborhood as to what was taking place. In the light of good judgment, the program was shelved.

The rumor was of great impact. Political forces made every attempt to change two names, the Hamburg Savings Bank and Hamburg Avenue in Brooklyn. They were only successful in changing Hamburg Avenue to Wilson Avenue. The bank retained its name through the years, until it merged recently with the Greenpoint Savings Bank.

My parents decided that I take violin lessons. It so happened that the church choir master, a Mr. Blatz, in addition to his church duties, taught piano and violin lessons from his home. The cost was a reasonable one at fifty cents an hour, considered a good price at the time.

I progressed nicely and played solo violin selections accompanied by my teacher at various parish functions. On one occasion I believe it was Halloween when I was scheduled to perform. Many of my schoolmates, including me, were present a little early before adult supervision arrived. Those present became a little unruly, and whatever could be thrown was thrown. I, very anxious to perform, had my violin under my arm, all tuned awaiting my cue. One of my pals threw a janitorial-style push broom, in javelin-style that struck my violin, leaving its neck dangling from its body. This catastrophe ended any attempt to perform. To make a long story short, when nuns and supervisors arrived, the culprit was identified and all matters ended amicably. The repairs were paid for by the boy's parents, but the party continued sans my virtuoso talent displayed.

During the last grade summer vacation, it was customary for youngsters to engage in some kind of summer working program, but with me being age fourteen at the time, a permit was required, which was obtained. I remember traveling to Manhattan to work as a page boy for the Title Guarantee and Trust Co. at 176 Broadway in lower Manhattan. My salary was eight dollars per week, a windfall at this time and a lasting experience for me.

About ten youngsters all about the same age sat on a bench in the main lobby with a supervisor, in school fashion style seated at a desk in control. A large panel board fitted with a cluster of lights operated so that when one blinked, the youth next in turn was told where to go to accomplish his mission. This was my introduction to the working world.

My newly arrived sister Agnes was progressing nicely. Aside from becoming friends, I was given responsibility for certain home chores. This included store shopping and at times minding my sister. Time for elementary grade-school graduation was approaching.

My classmates and I advanced not only in knowledge but in years. Recalling earlier, I had a fight in the school alley with one of my classmates. Well, apparently ill feelings were still kept fresh in his mind. Rounding the corner of Catalpa and Onderdonk Avenues, en route home, I was attacked by him and another lad unknown to me. Unfortunately, he had a safety razor blade in his hand that put a three-inch gash in my left cheek to the ear. The flow of blood ended the fight and I ran home, to tell my mom. When I arrived home, I could see the reflection of my face in the door glass panel and it was horrible. I cannot describe my mom's reaction. Fortunately, she was able to contact Dr. Kemp, who put three sutures to close the wound. My parents met with my assailants, and all matters both financial and disciplinary were taken care of.

During my grade-school years, I received my First Holy Communion and was confirmed. My dad's brothers, Louis and Frank, were my sponsors.

All through these years, at times, my mom and dad played host and hostess to many family gatherings, including their friends. I felt so sorry for my mom, for she tried so hard to be the gracious hostess. At clean-up time, all the womenfolk pitched in to lend a helping hand. I graduated from St. Mathias and was enrolled at Newton High School, in Elmhurst, a short ride from home by trolley. I enrolled in a technical course that included: shop work, chemistry; mechanical drawing, etc.

Going from a parochial school to a public high school, to me, was the difference between night and day. It seemed cold and impersonal. Much time was lost marching through corridors to reach the next class with a different teacher in charge. The personal touch that I was accustomed to was missing.

No one classroom or teacher was assigned. When the session bell sounded, you would proceed to your next classroom and new teacher. The corridors were monitored to see that it all took place in orderly fashion.

My violin lessons continued along with much practice. Blessed events added to the family. On January 3, 1920, we welcomed my sister Genevieve, and Geraldine on October 24, 1921. With three sisters my responsibilities at home increased. I could be seen pushing a baby carriage with a sister holding each side. God forbid that one fell; I was held accountable, to the extent that I was careless in watching over them.

I, still in the category of a youngster, was assigned weekly tasks at home of dusting and washing windows. I remember sitting on the ledge, six stories above the ground to get the job done. Violin practice and homework were all part of my agenda. When it came time for me to play, the time was limited. My sisters would act up because I was not caring for them.

My dad was a tough taskmaster. The fear that I had of him was never eased to the point where he would take me for a walk that would lessen the work stress on my mom. A ball game was out of the question. If I played marbles, I was wasting my time. Many a time, I was punished for things that happened. I forgive him, bless his soul, for he never enjoyed the pleasures of childhood.

One day I was told that we were moving to Middle Village on Admiral Avenue, 64-41 to be exact. This was a new development of two-story homes, nicknamed "Yaphank."

Author's three sisters, left to right: Genevieve, Geraldine, and Agnes. Insert: the author. Location: Queens, New York.

A great deal of work was required for this move. My sisters attending St. Mathias School were now transferred to the Our Lady of the Miraculous Medal School. I was still at Newton High. Certain adjustments were made by me, for I maintained contacts with my old classmates. At St. Mathias, a good recreational room was available for pool, cards, etc., with a curfew set at ten P.M.

During all these years, my dad was promoted to Engineer in the New York City Fire Department, a rank held only by a few, mainly by men who worked the fire boats. Later, he was successful and was promoted to lieutenant and assigned to Engine Company 222, Quincy Street, in the Bedford Stuyvesant section of Brooklyn.

Working conditions in the Fire Department at this time were far different from what they are today. Many a time when my dad worked twenty-four hours, my mom would prepare a lunch bucket, easily reheated, a regular home-cooked meal that I would bring to him at the fire house. This gave me the opportunity to spend a few hours with my dad. I got to know most of the men. Many times my dad was kidded on how well his spouse took care of him. I enjoyed myself there, because at that time, horses pulled the engines to the fire scene. One horse, in particular, spotted like a Dalmatian was my choice and favorite.

When gongs sounded, the horses seemed to know which ones they would respond to and they became restless in their stalls. If so, with a push of a button, by the man-on-watch, chains were lowered from the ceiling and each horse would proceed to his assigned position at the fire truck. Truly a picture of precision. When all were harnessed, it was a picture to see the horses racing to the scene of the fire.

If it was a worker, meaning a fire and not a false alarm, the horses were always under control, while the men worked. Relating this story today it seems so primitive compared to the streamlined, sophisticated apparatus in use today.

The fire house, Engine Company 222, located on Quincy Street in Brooklyn, was at one time a bon-ton neighborhood of residential homes. Through the years, conditions changed. I remember street lamplighters, lighting each street light in turn by hand.

The bon-ton homes, now rooming houses, became houses of ill repute, assignation, where so-called Johns would check in with some chick, holding a small handbag to appear as a legitimate transaction. An hour or two later, the couple would exit the premises.

One summer day after visiting my dad, who was working a twenty-four hour shift, I decided to walk home rather than take the Gates Avenue trolley. It was quite a distance from home, but my being young, it posed no problem.

I walked the route of the trolley car and was now at Myrtle Avenue junction. On the corner of Myrtle and Gates Avenue was a pet shop with a window display of monkeys. To break the monotony of walking and to rest a while, I enjoyed and chuckled at the performances of the window display of monkeys.

Suddenly, I felt a tap on my shoulder. When I turned I faced a man much older than I, who appeared to be a laborer type, a hard-working man. He asked me about the lady whom I had been following all the way from Quincy Street. I didn't know or realize what he was talking about. He questioned me further and what he was asking, to me made no sense.

I finally told him my dad was a fire lieutenant at 222 Engine Company on Quincy Street, and that I was walking home from a visit with him, since he was on a twenty-four hour shift. I also added that I had no recollection of any woman whom he was referring to.

Hearing what I had to say seemed to soften his attitude, and he told me a sad story.

He believed and knew that his wife was cheating on him. This woman apparently left a premise on Quincy Street at the time I left the fire house and walked the same route that I did. This prompted him to tap my shoulder. He explained how hard he worked for her and showed me his hands. He realized that I was telling the truth, and I remember we parted with a handshake.

In retrospect, I was in a potentially dangerous situation, if this man had been quick tempered before he asked questions. My parents, when they learned of my experience and how it ended, breathed a sigh of relief.

We had several family gatherings with my dad's family, and his cousins, the Komoras, whose mom was sister to my dad's mom. Much planning went into these gatherings because of my dad's working schedule. Emil Komora, who was studying for the priesthood, was ordained on September 20, 1924. I at this time was enrolled at Newton High School. Somehow or other I became inspired by the fact that my cousin was headed for religious life.

I seriously dwelled on my cousin's choice in life. Actually I was never happy with study arrangements at Newton High. However, still playing violin, I thought that joining the school orchestra might shed a different light on my feelings. I don't remember if I played first or second violin, but I do remember on one occasion we played a concert at Carnegie Hall in Manhattan. The school orchestra must have been considered good, else it would never have experienced that opportunity.

My thoughts were still focused on the way of life that my cousin Emil had taken. Reviewing in my mind memories of my being an altar boy, I decided that I wanted to follow in my cousins footsteps and study for the priesthood.

I finished a semester at Newton High School and explained to my parents what I considered my new goal in life. I explained how the ordination of Father Emil Komora inspired me. It was not hard to sell my idea to my parents.

Arrangements were made through my parish, St. Mathias, and since my parents were of moderate means, I was all set to enter Cathedral College, a prep seminary for a five-year period at this time.

3

McAllister Navigation Company

I was assigned Father Hoffman of St. Mathias, as my sponsor, with instructions that my progress charts would be presented to him monthly. Without doubt this was a new ball game. At the time that I enrolled and started, there were some 120 students with like ambitions. The 120 candidates made up three classes of forty each according to size. The school was located at Washington and Atlantic Avenues in Brooklyn. Father Patrick Kinsella was the dean. The sessions ran from Monday through Saturday, with Thursdays off.

We were assigned to a classroom and our teachers, all priests from different parishes, came to this room for teaching purposes. The curriculum presented was intense and varied, consisting of Mathematics, Ancient History, English, Latin, Greek, Religion, etc. Each subject was taught by a different priest, who in turn assigned homework to meet his needs. The homework assignments were heavy. The school facilities were limited except for handball courts and a gym, used for basketball. With great ambition, I faced this new schooling with a different attitude from the one I had at Newton High. The priest instructors were well informed on their subjects, which they delivered well. It appeared well organized, and I felt that I was off to a good start.

It took me a good while to adjust to this new scholastic program by comparison with Newton High School. The priests assigned, robed in their cassocks, plus their Roman collars, added dignity to the scene. It was interesting to study the personality of each priest and how he presented his subject matter. I made every effort not only to absorb all of the teachings but to retain what I learned.

Since there were 120 freshmen, it was difficult to get to know all. They were divided into three classes, located in three areas of the building.

The building in itself was not a spacious structure. The students could enjoy the courtyard, when at times, priests would engage in a game of handball. The gym was of regulation size to accommodate competition with other schools. During the holy seasons, an altar was always provided for, so as to be able to celebrate Masses. Interest in sports knows no limits, so when our school basketball team played Seton Hall at our court, or any other school team, our gym was packed with students. At times, students of the visiting team attended as spectators to lend support for their home team.

At this writing, I can well remember a senior student named Graham, an excellent player, who years later after ordination was assigned to my parish, Our Lady of Mercy in Forest Hills.

Getting used to Thursday as being my day off posed no problem. Attending classes on Saturday took a little time to get used to. In general everything was so well organized that in no time we were just rolling along.

I found myself visiting Barnes and Noble bookstore, purchasing "trots," to assist me in the literal translation of our Latin and Greek texts, which always were part of our home study.

Annually the school published a yearbook upon the

graduation of the senior class, which represented the completion of a five-year program. To help swell the pages of this journal, a competition was held among the 120 freshmen classes. The competition was that the one who obtained the most ads for the journal, would win a baseball fielder's glove.

Full of great ambition and energy, I accepted this offer as a challenge. I at that time, living with my family in Middle Village, an area studded with many companies that supplied monumental memorials for family graves, targeted these companies for my solicitations. When management learned of the reason for my visits, I had no problem and received all sizes of ads with a contract that finalized the transaction. A deadline was set. My tally sheet, at school, exceeded by far those of my classmates. The net results were that I was presented with a well-appreciated fielder's glove.

During my vacation periods, via my dad, I managed to get a job, as a purser, with the McAllister Steamship Company, at 24 State Street in Manhattan. I understood that they seemed to welcome prep seminarians. This company ran excursion pleasure boats from Battery Park to Bear Mountain in upper New York State. As a purser, I was to sell tickets on the boat, a financial responsibility at age fifteen.

Their fleet consisted of four boats: the *Steamer Bear Mountain;* the *Claremont;* the *Ontiora;* and the *Favorite.* Their capacity ran from 300 for the *Favorite* to 3,000 for the *Claremont.* The *Steamer Bear Mountain* usually doubled each day with a moonlight sail in the evening. Dan F. McAllister was the boss, a man of tall frame. He always could be recognized by his rolling a cigar in his mouth from left to right side and vice versa, for he was a dry smoker. When any of his fleet was taking on passengers,

S.S. *Claremont* in background. The author and office manager at Bear Mountain.

he could be seen with Buck O'Neill, the Battery Park Dock Master, supervising conditions, while one of his office men was busy clocking the number of passengers going aboard. I understand that Dan, whom they called "D.F.," had two brothers. One was in the fuel business while the other handled tug boats for commercial boating in the river.

My day started at eight A.M., after picking up a uniform-type marine hat at the office. Anyone of the boats could have been my assignment that, when with full capacity, left for Bear Mountain, a scenic forty-five-mile cruise up the Hudson River. A round-trip adult ticket was sixty cents; fifty cents for one way. Children's tickets were thirty cents a round trip, and twenty-five cents one way. I started out with a cigar box, holding enough cash to begin the day.

Each boat in the fleet had a good-size band for dancing and enjoyment. It played throughout the day. On leaving the Battery, passing Pier A where the fire boat was moored, the band would always play MAGGIE, getting a return salute from the firemen. A growing feeling told me that I was going to like this job, for the boats and water had always fascinated me.

It was a seven-day-a-week job. Working hours meant nothing, all for one hundred dollars per month, plus dining-room meals with the ship's officers. On July Fourth, and weekends in mid-summer, the entire fleet would visit Bear Mountain. If I were on the first boat that left the Battery at nine A.M., and passenger traffic was heavy, I would be reassigned to leave Bear Mountain on the seven-thirty P.M. boat, arriving back at Battery Park about ten-thirty P.M., or later, depending on the tide.

I had the pleasure of working with two older seminarians, who later in years were ordained priests. One

The crew, all two-fisted men of the S.S. *Ontiora* at Bear Mountain. "Slim" centered in photo, with, from left: a crewmember, the cook, an office manager, and William McAllister. S.S. *Claremont* in background.

was a Father Ambrose McGowan and a Father William McAllister, no relation to the company.

Since my working hours were long and unpredictable, I arranged to use a stateroom on the S.S. *Ontiora* as my second home, returning home for fresh clothes as needed.

All of the fleet tied up at the Vulcan Iron Works in Jersey City, in the vicinity of the waterfront landmark of the Colgate Clock. Adjacent to these docks were railroad yards dimly lighted with an eerie bluish glare. While the fleet used this location, they in turn were not easily accessible. To get from one boat to another, one had to travel cautiously between railroad cars.

I got to know not only all of the ship's officers, but the deck crews. One day one of the pilots who knew of my sleeping on the *Ontiora* questioned me about this practice. He indicated that it was a dangerous area and reached into his pocket to show me a hand gun that he always carried when traveling the area. Learning of this, I was extremely careful when moving about in this area.

Most of the ship's officers, I understand, were retired New York State apple orchard farmers. They were all licensed by the U.S. Department of Commerce and worked only during the summer seasons. The deck crews were rough and tumble characters, all likable, who were beachcombers in California in the wintertime.

I assume that the oldest boat in the McAllister fleet was the S.S. *Ontiora,* with a capacity of about 2,500. It was a coal burner and side-wheeler. The top deck, called the poop-deck, was the prime place to sun oneself, but it had its disadvantages. When the men in the engine room fired the boilers, those sunning themselves were covered with soot blown from the stacks of the ship. The ship, although meeting all regulations for seaworthiness, was of

The author with one of the crew of the S.S. *Ontiora* at Bear Mountain.

The McAllister fleet, moored at their winter home at Bear Mountain, New York, December 1926.

such vintage that it did not have automatic stability ballast tanks.

Instead a clinometer pendulum was installed on a central beam, forward of mid-ship. This instrument listed the degree of list that the ship was riding to. When under way two crew members were always on watch at this point. When too great a list existed, these two crew members would roll 100-pound barrels of sand from port to starboard and vice versa, depending on the clinometer reading. This rolling of barrels usually took place when the ship was cruising through Haverstraw Bay, one of the widest areas of the Hudson River.

Along the shoreline on the Jersey side were campers. The Chris-Craft motor boat was apparently in vogue at this time. They would come out and circle the boat. Curiosity caused the passengers to move from port to starboard and vice versa, putting these two crew men in action, rolling barrels for greater stability. I have witnessed this boat with full capacity and little freeboard ship water that ran across the deck to exit on the other side. Passing through this point, some twenty to twenty-four barrels were always in motion for stability.

One of the deck hands, an Irishman with eyebrows that looked like wire and a dark-shaven face, became one of my friends. In conversation I learned that he had just been released from Sing Sing on a manslaughter charge, resulting from the death of the man with whom he had been fighting.

During my second summer, I dealt with the same officers and deck-hands, which made it more pleasant. Each had tall stories to relate. At that time, I was teamed up with another lad, John King. He too was working as a purser. He was a Fordham law student, who became my lifelong friend.

Bear Mountain was a beautiful state park, with a variety of means to picnic and relax. After the passengers disembarked, I would tally my receipts and head for the lake and the row boats that I had access to. Daily I had the opportunity to row some two or three hours before getting back to my station. Keep in mind that someone was always at the boat to answer questions.

On occasion while cruising, the skipper would invite me up to the pilot house. The pilot would turn the helm over to me, and under his supervision, I was steering the boat. I remember sounding one long blast signal as we came to a bend in the river.

One day, just by coincidence, two rival New York mobs booked passage on the same boat. It did not take too long for either mob to recognize this dilemma. After leaving the 132nd Street Pier, a fight broke out, involving both mobs. The crew and I, being part of the crew, were called into action. The captain signaled for help, and the boat returned to the 132nd Street Pier where the police took over. It took a while before we resumed our travel.

During the height of the summer, when many New Yorkers with their families wanted to enjoy cool breezes, they took the cruise up the Hudson River to Bear Mountain. A more expensive steamship line, the Hudson River Day Line, would make a stop at Indian Point, just below Bear Mountain on the east side of the river.

On many occasions, the McAllister Line chartered extra boats over weekends in the height of the season, Memorial Day, and July Fourth, to take care of the overflow: the *Mobjack;* the *Blue Bird;* the *Steamer Belle Island;* the *Renssalear,* and the *Trojan.* Once they chartered the *Mandalay,* owned by the Diamond Company, formerly a ship for conveying railroad cars; that is why its bow and stern were rounded like a ferryboat, with the top or poop-deck off limits for passengers. I had worked on all of them, yet for record, I had never set foot on Ellis Island or the Statue of Liberty, yet one of our fleet, the S.S. *Favorite* made daily trips.

One evening, in my third year, I was selling tickets at 132nd Street Pier for the moonlight sail. A supervisor working out of the office paid me a visit. He suggested, instead of my returning to the office, he would deliver my receipts. I agreed to this, for now I could go straight home. Lo and behold, the next day, I learned that he, upon entering the State Street building, was held up. Fortunately, he was not injured. I had a good Guardian Angel and said a prayer of thanks. This brought to mind that on many a day, during my first two summers, I would carry my receipts, some three thousand dollars, in a cigar box crossing Battery Park to the State Street office. The office was open twenty-four hours daily, since they had a dispatcher handling tug-boat assignments.

Summer passed quickly and school was again in session. I had many stories to tell my classmates, but I guess in some instances they fell on deaf ears. School was no piece of cake. I found myself doing homework well after bedtime. My report cards were presented to my sponsor, Father Hoffman. He reviewed them and always had a word of encouragement for me.

With my experience in the working world, I must have appeared a little more mature than my fellow-classmates. Sometimes I felt if my name had been Kelly or O'Brien, I would have fared better with my teachers. Then too, this may only have been a figment of my imagination.

The years rolled by. At one time my three sisters, each in turn, was suffering from measles. To avoid my exposure to this situation, arrangements were made that I live with my cousins, the Komoras. They lived in Yorkville section of Manhattan on Eighty-Fourth Street. There were five in the family, including their mom and dad.

Emil, the priest who inspired my change of course in life, was ordained September 20, 1924. He was assigned to St. Joseph's Parish at 125th Street and Morningside Avenue in Manhattan. Paul was married, which left Anna, Irene, and Edward, with Mom and Pop in charge. Now, I had a greater distance to travel via the Third Avenue "EL" to arrive at my school in Brooklyn, as per schedule.

I have no recollection as to how long I stayed there, but I remember ice-skating in Central Park, visiting the Museum of Art on Fifth Avenue and swimming in a city pool on Eighty-Sixth Street overlooking the East River. Again, I have no recollection as to when I returned home to my regular schedule. Somehow or other, a sour attitude built up toward my schooling, and to explain this to my parents was difficult, but I called it quits, leaving Cathedral College in my fourth year.

I imagine, still in the youngster category, being exposed to the working forces of the world, resulted in my having a different attitude with respect to my future. I now wanted to work hard, and I mean laborious work.

I read want ads and visited a few locations for interview without results. My parents without doubt were disappointed with my decision. Jobs were hard to come by. My dad at times was difficult to understand, for now I had quit school and was unemployed.

4

Triangle Conduit, Laborious Work

Keeping contact with some of my school chums, I learned that one was a plumber's helper, another worked on Wall Street, while another worked on an oil tanker ferrying to New Orleans.

Things were so bad that I looked at the bulletin boards of employment agencies along Sixth Avenue in Manhattan. The "EL" was still operating. Dishwashers seemed to be available in one-arm restaurants. Mulling over my opportunities, I drew the line at these offerings.

Familiar with the waterfront to some degree, Pier 17 at the Hudson River was used as a shape-up point by the New York Central Railroad. In the morning, groups would assemble, hoping to be selected for some assignment on one of their tugs. There were no unions at this time, so I blended in with others, mostly of foreign extraction, wearing working garb.

I was selected for five dollars per day to work on one of their sea-going tugs. My first assignment was to be an oiler in the engine room. I was shown how and when to use the long-nosed oil can. It not only was a hairy job, but the heat was over 100 degrees. I bargained with one who seemed to be in charge and I was sent up on deck.

I had no idea as to where we were going, but leaving the lower New York Bay, we were headed for the

Gowanus Canal to tow a barge with a cargo of bananas. I watched the deck hands' precision performance in handling lines, in the tie-up of the barge to the tug, a masterful display of seamanship. As the lines became taut, if one were not careful, one could lose an arm or leg if caught in the process.

On another occasion we were headed for the steamer's quarantine anchorage area in lower New York's Bay. This move was made to receive sacks of mail from ships that just returned from trans-Atlantic voyages. I repeat, there were no unions and whether you worked eight or sixteen hours, your pay was five dollars. The tug would expertly tie up alongside the ship and a shute was set up, carrying the sacks to the deck of the tug. Relieving some dozen ships of their mail, we returned to Pier 17 and were paid off.

I got a good taste of this type of work that prompted me to make other decisions for my future.

In the meantime, through contacts with a neighbor friend, a husky German lad, I was successful in getting a longshore-type job unloading railroad freight cars for the Triangle Conduit Company in Middle Village, Queens. As I remember it was a seven-thirty A.M. to five P.M. job paying twenty-two dollars per week. I wanted to work hard, and I found my goal.

The Triangle Conduit and Cable Company was actually a factory where all types of electrical conduit and cable were manufactured. A railroad siding entered their yard, where cars loaded with various materials used in manufacturing would arrive daily.

Actually, I was working in the shipping department with about nine others. A few were of various ethnic backgrounds.

Two brothers were in charge to oversee and run the

place. The older brother was a real businessman, while the other, who usually worked with the help, liked to "nibble," but he still managed to do his share of the work under the supervision of his brother.

I wanted to work hard, and I got my wish. Cars that came in on the siding were loaded with all the necessary materials to operate this type of factory.

Steel coils, each a 100-pound weight, would be loaded on a hand truck. Ten such coils loaded on a hand truck was considered a load to be pushed to the designated bin for storage. This was all done by hand. A car could carry hundreds of these coils. This material was used for the manufacture of the flexible cable of all gauges.

Then too, metal piping all sizes at least 15 feet in length would make up a car's cargo. Pipes of this sort were used to house wiring for underground work, to protect the wires from corrosion. The smaller diameter pipes were tied in bundles of four or six and shoulder-carried to their respective bins for storage.

A distasteful task occurred when a car came in loaded with sheets of rubber, used for insulation. These sheets were well powdered to keep them from sticking together. As I view it today, this was hazardous work. No mask was worn or even suggested. When this job was completed, those who participated were covered from head to foot with white powder. I know that some of this must have been inhaled. As a result, I chewed tobacco to keep my throat moist. These sheets were placed on a platform. A hand-operated machine would convey the load to the storage bin, where again manual work took care of the storing.

My German pal and I usually worked together. All of the staff did their share of work. On occasion the boss would select one of the men to assist on truck deliveries.

Meal time was one half hour. I would take advantage of this time by resting on the top of the railroad car, propping myself in such a way that I would not roll off and fall to the ground.

A school chum, an altar boy from St. Mathias, now a Fordham law student, asked if I could get him a job for the summer so he could harden up for the football team. The boss took him on with no problem. My friend Dom Tosti admitted that it was hard work that met his needs.

When I received my pay each week, twenty-two dollars, I gave it to my parents. They in turn gave me enough for car fare and lunch. This was a must, for I could not keep my salary. My boss approached me one day and informed me that I was going to receive an increase of one dollar in my pay. I did not reveal this to my dad and I kept the extra dollar. I have no idea how this happened, but I learned later that my dad must have paid a visit to my boss and learned that I got an increase of one dollar. Some time later I learned through conversation with my dad that he knew of my increase and that I was keeping the money. As I mentioned before, my dad was a tough taskmaster from the old school, feeling that children should help support their families.

I worked for Triangle Company for about a year and a half. During all these years, I kept contact with John King, my lifelong friend, who worked with me on the McAllister fleet. I confessed that I was fed up with this kind of hard work. John insisted that I return to school to obtain my full educational credits. I mulled over this move for a while and wondered what response or cooperation I would get from my parents.

At what I thought was the appropriate time, I broke the news to my parents, that I wanted to return to school to obtain my full credits. No immediate answer was received.

Shortly thereafter I was enrolled at St. Augustine's Academy, an all-male school, run by Christian Brothers in Brooklyn. I learned that my previous school credits were far more than was required. In order to comply with school regulation, I had to select calculus to fulfill credits for a year of study.

School was now my ambition, having experienced some of the world's bitterness.

5

St. Augustine's Academy

A Brother Patrick was the Dean. I learned that he was as former dean of a reform school. He was a black beady-eyed man, whose eyes seemed to pierce you when in conversation.

There I found myself with men my age, but not as worldly wise or experienced. I enjoyed my change-over. An interesting note, *The Loughlin Lance Journal,* commencement number 1929, indicated that my first appearance among my classmates was responsible for various and contradictory conjectures concerning me. All the teachers were brothers except for the English teacher, a lay person, Mr. Thomas A. Murphy. I enjoyed being back again carrying books under my arm after a few worldly encounters.

All through these years, my sisters were advancing in age and loveliness. For some reason, via the doctor, they, including me, were prone to getting sore throats. On advice of the doctor, an appointment was made with the Brooklyn Eye, Nose, and Throat Hospital on Greene Avenue in Brooklyn to have all our tonsils removed on the same day.

My sisters were all given an anesthesia, while I had undergone the operation with a local medication. We all spent one night at the hospital and returned home the next day. The period of recovery was interesting to note. My youngest sister was ready to eat, other than ice cream in one week. The next in turn took two weeks, while the third sister took a three-week period for recovery. I, being the oldest, took one month to recover and resume normal activities.

This action kept me from school for one month. As I look back at this situation, it was not a smart move to have me included in this family maneuver.

At school the one study that I needed to fulfill credits for the school semester was calculus. Returning to school, I, on my own, dropped attending this session, because of my month's absence. I now devoted my time to my other studies.

The dean, Brother Patrick, had me in his office, read the riot act to me, and asked "With whose permission did you drop this study?" I answered that it was my decision. He replied that by me taking this action my school requirements will not have been met and my graduation will become questionable. I left his office with tongue in cheek. I was determined to catch up on what I had missed.

Annually the school via the English professor, Mr. Murphy, would select plays for a school performance as part of his curriculum. This presented a new challenge to me, for I always had dreamt of some day playing a part in one of Shakespeare's masterpieces.

With the words of the dean ringing in my ears, I was determined to work harder to redeem myself.

The school was celebrating some special function, and the English professor decided to put on a one-act play for the occasion. He chose an English play, titled *The Ghost of Jerry Bundler*. I do not recall its author, but somewhere, buried in my files, I have a copy.

Auditions were held to play the lead. I was extremely satisfied when I learned, that I had been selected. It was an English play and under the expert direction of the English professor, I was speaking with a Cockney accent. As I remember there was only one performance and from all reports, it went well.

Graduation time was drawing near, and preparations were being made to stage a Broadway show, with the students as actors. This production was to be held before graduation, and there was no time to be lost. All financial receipts were for the benefit of the school.

I learned that the Broadway play, *The Show-Off,* was selected. A comedy-classic well known, playing the legitimate theater and the movies with Jackie Gleason, playing the lead, a man of many talents.

Auditions were held to play the lead as "Aubrey Piper." About a dozen class mates responded to the call. Each student was given the opportunity to display his talents. In the final decision, I was selected to play the lead of Aubrey Piper. Being an all-male school an invite was sent to St. Joseph's Business School, an all-girl school, not too far distant, to entice their female students to audition for the female characters. This invite was welcomed and several good-lookers appeared for the audition. It did not take too long before we had a full cast ready for rehearsal. A gal by the name of Eulalia Jones was selected to be my show-wife.

Under the professional guidance of our English professor, we rehearsed and rehearsed.

A great deal of publicity was given to this school project. Tickets were sold in such numbers that the play was scheduled for three occasions, to satisfy and meet the demands of the numbers of tickets sold. Each evening the auditorium was solid with parents, relatives, and friends.

It was a success and to me a self-gratification since I was playing the lead. My mind now drifted to perhaps selecting an acting career for a livelihood.

A quote from *The Loughlin Lance,* the commencement journal, 1929, "He played the part of Aubrey Piper in *The Show-Off,* to perfection before three separate audiences and won round after round of applause."

The school in appreciation for the success of the play, had our English professor, coach and director, invite the entire cast to a "night on the town" with dinner at a New York Hotel in the vicinity of Greely Square. We all felt like stars and had an enjoyable dinner.

Our dinner invite ended in the early evening hours. Our coach told us that we were now on our own; he left for home.

Since it was early evening, I suggested taking a Fifth Avenue bus, a double-decker, and head for Washington Square Park to sight-see in the Village. There was no hesitation in thinking out my suggestion, and a full vote of yes was given.

We were now all en route on the bus to the famous Washington Arch, the landmark to the Village. I won't say that the Village to me was old hat, but my friends seemed to enjoy what they saw. No, we did not stop at any watering holes. Our excursion was all over and above board.

Having satisfied our curiosity and now past our bedtime, we decided to break up and head for home. I playing the gentleman, escorted my play-wife to her home in Brooklyn.

We arrived in the neighborhood; all new to me, hence she directed our travel. The time was in the area of twelve-thirty A.M. As we approached her home, her father, looking much disturbed in the night's darkness, in a loud tone asked, "Why are you so late?" I tried to explain, but my voice fell on deaf ears. This brief encounter more or less spoiled the evening, and I left for home.

On my return to school the next day, I learned that her dad checked with the school, wondering what type of a lad I was. Yes, the dean called me in for an explanation. Apparently, I was the only one of the group to have experienced this type of situation, for no remarks were heard at any time later.

If after the suggestion that I had made earlier, namely the Village trip, someone had indicated that they had a return-home curfew, this unpleasant situation would never have happened. As for our female cast from St. Joseph's, I don't believe that any of the male cast had ever been in contact with or even seen them since. Hopefully it was a forgotten issue, with pleasant memories.

A graduation date was set with all the trimmings of Cap and Gown. I would not think of asking my dad to cover the expense. As a result, a few days before graduation, with a cigarette in my hand, I rang the door bell to the Brothers' residence. Brother Patrick answered and asked me what I wanted. I explained that I would not be present on graduation night, if it were possible to get my diploma now. In no short terms and piercing eyes, he said, "We don't smoke here and visitors don't smoke," and he shut the door in my face.

I flipped the butt into the street and rang the door bell again. There was no response. I have no recollection of what happened after this. I admit now that my conduct was bold and not proper. The Dean, Brother Patrick, was most forgiving, for I received my diploma the night after the formal graduation took place.

My performance in playing the lead three nights in *The Show-Off* must have softened his heart, for he realized how hard I worked to make it all a success. The final curtain had now fallen on my school years.

The accolades that I received for my performance stayed with me a long time. I even gave thought to following an acting career. I gave thought to enrolling at the Academy of Dramatic Arts, but that was a costly move and I knew that my family would not agree.

The year was 1929, when the economy started to wane and jobs were hard to come by. I even joined the Catholic Actor's Guild and attended several meetings, hoping to get some leads.

6

Public National Bank & Trust Company

With acting still on my mind, I visited several Broadway theatrical agencies. While someone was always in attendance, the summer session reflected a real lull. *Variety* was the theatrical newspaper, and I made every effort to obtain information and leads from it. Summer stock companies usually popped up, playing rural areas at this time of the year. I thought if I could connect with one, it would be a schooling for me. At the moment I felt that I was up a cul-de-sac.

My lifelong friend John King, whom I met working the McAllister fleet, always found time for getting together to hash things over. He still was in law school at Fordham, yet we managed to dump a few at McSorley's Ale House on Seventh Street off the Bowery, exchanging views as to what our crystal ball would tell us about our future. Incidentally, this pub, at this time, was off-limits to females. You could cut the smoke with a knife, and the free lunch table was out of this world. I always felt at home in this place, for it was just around the corner from my birthplace.

It was tough going in those Depression years, and while I had chores at home with three sisters, I did my best to not become a burden since I was unemployed.

Times were so bad in the business world, that my dad, although working Civil Service as a Fire Lieutenant, worked quite a while on what was referred to "pay-less furloughs." I don't recall how this came about, but I learned of a job in banks, referred to as "Rack Department," that worked at night. Investigating this lead further, I found out that this was the crew that tallied all the accounts from branch offices and finished each day by dropping off the material at the Federal Reserve Bank on Maiden Lane, in Manhattan.

I applied for this type of position at the Public National Bank & Trust Company at its main office at William and Liberty Streets in Manhattan. I was interviewed by a man from personnel and taken to a basement office, stacked with old-type Burroughs hand-operated adding machines and given a batch of checks to add. I took the checks and after a quick survey of the keys, I started to record the amounts by pulling a handle. In my so-called test performance, I only recoded the dollar amounts, ignoring the change. The person supervising and evaluating my performance called to my attention that I was not recording the change amounts. Thinking quickly, I responded, "Yes, I know, for I thought you just wanted a display of my familiarity with the machine." I was hired and my hours at this main office started at six P.M., including Saturdays, since all banks then were open until one P.M. My starting salary was twenty-five dollars per week.

On my first night, I met my boss, whose name incidentally was Gerald Klein, no relative, and a working staff of about sixteen men. The department was divided into four sections, each with its own crew.

Two bank messengers, daily would pick up the checks in Brooklyn and Manhattan, where some fifty branch offices were located. All of these checks were processed by the particular branch and weighed at the main office. Our job was to tally all the checks and balance with the amounts recorded at the branches. In the area of 2:00 A.M., we were en route to the Federal Reserve on Maiden Lane.

The period of each month from the 10th to the 15th, the day's business of each of the branches was extremely heavy, the reason being, Bonds and Investments paid off, during this period. As I mentioned before, all the checks were weighed. During these periods it was nothing to have all weighing, in the neighborhood of one-hundred pounds. What did this mean? It meant that the crew would come in at three P.M., and work until the day's receipts were finished and results proven accurate.

I remember coming to work at three P.M., during this period on a Saturday and leaving for home at two P.M., Sunday afternoon. There was no overtime or supper money. Each in turn left with bleary eyes from looking at figures and checking tapes when totals did not tally.

As I said, jobs were hard to come by. As a result I remember working with five lawyers, who worked their offices in the day and then worked this night shift. In our working group, there was a theatrical performer who could be found plying Broadway in the daytime looking for work.

In the Transit Department, consisting of out-of-town checks, a man would sit feeding a Recordack machine that would take a picture of the face of the check and on the second application the endorsement. The film for each day's recording, 8mm rolls, were delivered to Kodak Company on East Twenty-Third Street in Manhattan for development.

Depending on when each day's work was finished, I

would usually get home about three A.M. I lived on Admiral Avenue at this time with family in Middle Village at 64-41. I had what they called a hall room over the porch. When my dad rented the apartment upstairs and the tenant did not fire their coal furnace, there was no heat in this room. In the wintertime I had to bundle up to keep warm. This problem was corrected when my dad took over the second floor, two front rooms for my three sisters, he kept both furnaces banked for the night.

On Saturdays when my day's work at the bank ended rather early, I would attend a two A.M., Sunday Mass at St. Andrews R.C. Church on Duane Street just off Chambers Street. It was known as the Printer's Mass, because of the different newspaper plants operating in this area of downtown Manhattan. My next turn to my working shift was six P.M., on Monday evening.

When my friends heard that I was working in a bank at night, they immediately had me in the position of doing janitorial services. The "Rack Department" was well known in banking circles although the average person had no knowledge of its existence.

The bank had some fifty branches. Two messengers would pick up the day's work of each branch and deliver it to the main office at William and Liberty Street. Keep in mind that each branch had tallied their business transactions for the day and here is where all the days work was consolidated, totaled for accuracy, before delivering it to the Federal Reserve Bank at Maiden Lane.

With the poor economy, this consolidation of work afforded the main office to evaluate each of its branches for accuracy, volume, and productivity.

I was more than happy to be employed. In a short period of time, I got to know all sixteen men rather well. I evaluated each in turn as to their backgrounds and how long a time that they held this position. There were no grades, for all did the same work, except for the boss Mr. Klein, no relative, who supervised the operation.

Working nights, by necessity, put a dent in my social activities. Yet, I did manage to keep up with my old and newly acquired friends. Each night at work was like playing the same old record over and over. It became routine. Handling checks drawn on different banks, countrywide was a good lesson in geography. Considering that these were hard times, when a check for five thousand dollars surfaced, it represented a lot of money. Interesting to note that some checks were signed with an X plus a signature.

After leaving the "EL" station walking down Nassau Street, it was in itself a study to see people scurrying to the subway after finishing their day's work and here I was just about to start mine.

I realized that while we were an important cog in the wheel of the banking world, we were unknown as a group and chances of furthering one's goal were nil. A few of my co-workers, very competent, had been handling this job for ten or more years.

I was still living at home with my parents and sisters, but after hard bargaining, my financial condition changed and to some degree I felt more independent.

Days and weeks passed quickly. When we finished at two A.M., that was considered normal. During the heavy times of the month, the tenth to the fifteenth, five or six A.M. was considered normal. There were times during this poor economy period when the receipts from the branches were light. Via good management by our boss, we rarely ever left before two A.M., in the light of good judgment. The reasons were obvious.

To this day, I guess that I have always been a night

person. With my mind still dreaming of a theatrical career, I learned that one of my pals, a former altar boy, was working a Broadway show. I knew him fairly well from school, and I had a lot of questions to ask of him when we met.

I learned that he mastered his dancing, all types except ballet at the Tommy Nip's Studio on Broadway in the Roseland Dance building. My friend seemed most happy, for he pursued what he wanted and was now performing on Broadway.

My ambitions brought me to this studio, and after being interviewed, I signed up for lessons. This arrangement of attending dance school in daytime fit well, for I was working nights and my days were free.

7

Show Business—Broadway

I was impressed visiting this studio. It appeared that professionals as well as students male and female were engaged in some type of activity. Some were stretching their limbs on rails along the wall, while others were "hoofing" in front of mirrors that lined the walls. My bank work was six days per week because banks at this time were open a half-day on Saturdays. I arranged my dance instructions for afternoon sessions, three or four times per week, keeping in mind that a student was welcome at anytime for practice.

My instructor was Bobby Sanford, thin of frame, with wide-bottom trousers, the style at the time. Having watched him perform on occasion, he could sure "go to town" and sell his routine. I envisioned his talents rubbing off on me, hopefully. To be able to follow the beat of music was a must. What was considered "light on your feet" came from much practice. The "time step" in tap-dancing was my first introduction and challenge. This step was called a "Break," usually done after eight bars of music.

Many strenuous hours went into my practice both at the studio and at home, with and without music. The taps had to be loud and clear. One had to learn how to look relaxed during practice. After a period of time, your body movements would move freely just as when one was walking.

When time came to leave for work, I realized that my new goals had drained some of my energies. As a result, I had to adjust and ease into this program of dancing, working gently from the start. It was both a challenge and a dream, and I was determined to fulfill my ambitions. Weeks and months passed quickly. Bobby was an excellent instructor, who stressed style and performance. I now realized that I could do a routine with ease and follow the music, both regular and soft shoe.

I was so pleased with myself, for now I could do something that I had no dream of ever accomplishing.

On occasion, different vaudeville performers would just drop by for a visit to say hello or don a pair of tights and practice a routine. Being busy at both ends, work and dancing, time passed quickly. I did not reveal my ambitions to the men with whom I worked. I felt that this was a private matter.

One day at the studio, I learned that the Nip Studio was considering a stage show for the Paramount Publix Circuit. These contracts usually were made for fifty-two weeks, covering major cities in the United States and Canada. Then, too I learned that the studio was supplying the dancers. Having been tutored by Bobby Sanford and acquiring the status for entering the professional field as a dancer, I was given the opportunity to be one of the cast.

Six girls and six men were selected for the dancing segment of the show. Many thoughts were now running through my mind; I had a job with a bank and now was presented with the opportunity of working a show as a professional dancer. A decision had to be made. With tongue in cheek and great ambitions in mind, I handed in my resignation at the bank after working there for about one and a half years. My co-workers were surprised and all wished me well. I said that I would see them on Broadway.

I learned that the show was to be called, *The Lilliputians,* an idea I assume taken from *Gulliver's Travels.* The main dance was portraying diminutive people, the dancers squatting in Russian style, moving about to a beautiful choreographed routine. Then too, a tango, a waltz in high hat and tails plus a tap routine were also planned.

Before going into rehearsal, we learned that a British comedy, husband-and-wife team would headline the show. The "Three Jacks," a tap challenge group, an old time vaudeville act "Now and Then," plus Braille and Polo, exhibition Latin dancers filled the rest of the bill. We were now officially notified that we were going into rehearsal for at least a three-week period. A whole new life had started for me. For those of my group who had prior experience, rehearsals were "Old Hat." The gal assigned as my partner was Marion Wright. She was blonde, about 5′7″, physically attractive, with no problem with the art of dancing. The choreographer, Bobby, in my book was a genius. He stressed and got the precision he wanted in each routine. We all worked hard, anxiously awaiting the date of our opening night. After three intensive weeks of rehearsing, we learned that we would open in Boston.

This being my first professional appearance on stage, I tried to envision what my feelings would be on opening night. To my surprise when the pit band played our opening number, we made a flashing appearance on stage all hyped ready to perform. The footlights along the apron of the stage gave a glare that seemed to protect us from the

Show troupe of Spanish dancers, on the road. The author is at center.

audience. I will honestly say all performed well and we played to a full house.

Having broken the ice, each performance seemed to be done with greater ease and confidence. On our own, we evaluated the response from each audience and it was excellent.

After a week of entertaining Bostonians, our next show stop was Hartford, Connecticut. The usual morning rehearsal with the pit orchestra took place and like a race horse in the starting gate, we were ready to entertain the Hartford audiences. Again, this week's performances went without hitch, and we were now all looking forward to play the New York Paramount on Broadway, opening on Christmas Day. Aside from the holiday season being in the air and one's blood, we were all anxious to add to the Christmas spirit on Broadway.

The New York Paramount Theater to me was one of Broadway's finest. The Palace was the epitome to play for vaudeville acts. The Capitol was famous for theatrical headliner's appearances.

We arrived in New York about six A.M., and after breakfast, we went into rehearsal with the pit orchestra at eight A.M. I remember doing five shows on Christmas day. It was not an easy task, but when caught up into the Christmas spirit, it was a great pleasure. Being in New York, my hometown, gave me the opportunity to spend some time with my folks.

From audience response and reports, the show was a real entertainer. Most performances it played to a full house, considering the standing lines outside waiting to get in. The show, most entertainers disliked, yet the same energies were expended, was the dinner show. Peeking at the audience from the wings, many seats were empty and when applause was usually expected, it seemed as though the audience was sitting on their hands.

The Christmas week at the New York Paramount passed quickly. Our next stop was opening New Year's Day at the Brooklyn Paramount. Rudy Vallee was the headliner for the week. Remember the performer who used a megaphone crooning his love songs standing at the stage's apron? The stage door, normally crowded with stage-door "Johnnies," was now taken over by females of all sizes and ages, hoping to get a snap picture or an autograph.

The whole company easily fell into the routine, that when moving from one theater to the next, a rehearsal took place about eight A.M., on the day we were to perform.

Our next theater was the Stanley Theater in Newark, New Jersey. To me, it appeared to be a theater of long standing with a history of topnotch performers making their appearances there. An oddity, the stage was so high and the orchestra pit so low, it gave the performer the feeling of dancing on a cliff.

The headliner, the week we played there, was Louis Armstrong. The hallmark of his identification was his trumpet, that he could make talk, plus a handkerchief in his hand to wipe the perspiration from his brow. I remembered closing his act in a back bend, pivoting on his head, making a circle while playing his trumpet. A performance of this type in theatrical logo was a "show stopper."

I kept contact, via mail, with my family to up-date them as to where we would be playing next. Traveling to different cities each week, to me was quite an experience. Aside from knowing the theater we would be playing, we also knew the location of the hotel that would provide housing for the cast.

We played many of the major cities, Philadelphia, Pittsburgh, Toledo, Ashtabula, Ohio, etc., and found all audiences appreciative and receptive of our performances.

While in Chicago, I remembered the Loop and stayed at the Wacker Hotel in the area of the Chicago River. While we were always kept busy, practicing, we found time to get about and shop for needed items. We were enjoying our weekly schedules, when our stage manager revealed that some weeks had been cut from the original Paramount bookings. I imagine, based on information that he received from New York, he contacted Balaban and Katz, a theatrical agency in Chicago who picked up the slack and assigned us their bookings. We were sorry to hear this news, but happy that we were going to continue under new management.

An incident worthy of note, while in Chicago, I opened a savings account at the Garfield State Bank at Madison Street and Crawford Avenue, referred to as The Bank in the Heart of the Great West Side. What prompted this was, I did not know how long our stay would be, because of the termination of our Paramount Publix Contract. The economy was bad, in the midst of Depression years. This is why I feel Paramount terminated our contract. We were fortunate to have Balaban and Katz, in Chicago, take over our performance schedule.

Getting back to the Garfield Bank, as an incentive to open an account, a miniature chrome metal bank, shaped like a barrel, of good quality, three inches high was offered as a gift to new accounts. As I write this, I have the gift before me, some seventy years old with no signs of wear or deterioration. I have no recollection of what my balance was, but word was received that the Garfield

Bank went "belly-up," along with other financial institutions. A dollar in these years was worth a dollar. What little I had invested was completely lost.

Under our new contract, we played a one-night stand in Joliet, Illinois. This performance I feel was an audience feeler, to see how well we would be received.

One of our dancers, who in the past, doubled for Richard Dix, a look-alike, while in town had all his hair shaved off, with the hope of stimulating growth. This move in no way affected his performance, for we always wore a head dress. Dining in one of Joliet's restaurants on a Sunday, we overheard a child, close by, ask her dad if this man was a prisoner, since Joliet was known for its prison. We could not help but hear this question. Her remark was answered with a negative nod and a smile. While no conversation took place, it gave us a good chuckle.

Our stage manager, after getting the green light from our new boss, was now headed for the Fisher Theater in Detroit via the Big Four Railroad. About two A.M., while en route, we were all involved in a serious train accident running head-on into an oncoming train of forty-four boxcars. I folded up like an accordion in my bunk, with my head striking the partition part of the bunk. This happening brought everyone to their feet, including those playing cards in the wash room area, for they were thrown from their stools. The oncoming engine, I understand, was derailed.

I was informed later, that a fireman and engineer of the oncoming train had been killed. I have no idea as to what town we were near. Emergency crews were on the scene very quickly and worked to get the tracks clear so our travel could resume. We stopped at some town, where railroad officials boarded the train. Each one of our theater group was interviewed by some official.

Attorneys, I assume, were present and took part in the questioning. I was asked if I had sustained any injury. At the time of occurrence, my head hit the partition and at the moment it did not feel too bad. Since that was my only complaint, I received twenty-five dollars and asked to sign some papers, I assume, were releases. Others in the group were handled in like fashion. One of our group, who was playing cards, suffered a head injury when he struck a metal sink. He was given seventy-five dollars, on the spot after signing settlement papers.

Our group was fortunate, for no one seemed to have been hurt seriously. The tracks now having been cleared, we were again en route to Detroit. We were all told upon our arrival, where to go for further medical attention. The lad who struck his head on a sink, developed a few problems, and after receiving further attention, was given another one hundred dollars to close the case on his injury.

The Fisher Theater was located in the heart of the city, on a semi-circled area. I was given to understand that this showplace was only about two years old. This was the most attractive theater on the circuit for us. If I remember correctly, it was Egyptian style. The dressing rooms were lush compared to one theater we played, where both male and female shared a dressing room that was partitioned off.

Hell's Angels was the popular movie at this time, starring Jean Harlow. She incidentally was the headliner playing this theater, teamed up with actor Bill Powell, not the one who played *The Thin Man.* Stars usually close a production, such as this one. Hence, when they filled the main spot in the show, with spotlight on them, Bill Powell with his sax and Jean at his side danced to the

Ms. Jean Harlow, at the time starring in the movie *Hell's Angels,* and headliner at the Fisher Theatre in Detroit. Photo taken by the author.

tune of "Walking My Baby Back Home." It was a show-stopper.

Memories of the train accident remained with us. Before we left Detroit, each of our cast was given their final medical attention. In spite of all that happened, we enjoyed Detroit and we thanked our audiences for their generous applause.

Our next stop was St. Louis. I remember well, for I experienced a setback. Ligaments in both legs were strained due to the strenuous Lilliputian number. A cane became my best friend, and with medical attention, I was once again able to perform, on the theory that the show must go on. During my absence for a weeks' performance, five dance teams filled the bill nicely. I responded well, and with my partner, we filled the spot we vacated for one week.

We played a theater in Indianapolis, the name I don't remember. But when Sunday came, I do remember serving Mass at a local church, since no altar boys were present on the altar.

The priest celebrating Mass, in Latin, at this time was receptive to my presence. It had been a long time since my altar-boy days, but I answered in Latin, those prayers that I remembered. After Mass we had a nice chat, touching on many subjects. He was pleased to learn that I was a visitor in town, dancing in a Paramount show at one of the local playhouses. He gave me his blessing and left. I was pleased with myself, for what I did brought back pleasant memories and it sort of made my day.

The hotel that the cast was using as its home away from home, was of old vintage. I assume by this time it had been demolished and replaced by a modern type of building, either a residential or business.

One thing that I remember vividly about this hotel,

that deserves mentioning is that it was infested with cockroaches, the big ones, similar to the palmetto bug. Getting up at night to visit the commode and turning on a light, they were all over the floor. Walking in bare feet was an unpleasant experience. It reminded me of a place the troupe stayed at when we played a theater in Toronto. The playhouse was beautiful, but the housing facility was a second-class hotel. I remember going to bed at night wearing gloves, not to keep warm but to try to avoid bed bug bites. I remember burning an incense candle to try to freshen up the aroma in the place. Yet the troupe stayed there.

In spite of poor housing facilities, we all enjoyed playing Toronto. While on the subject of Canada, we all knew that Prohibition existed in the United States. Our touring and entertaining meant hard work. This was our profession and we loved every moment of it. Yes, on occasion playing the different cities, we met with similar groups and always managed to have a little party. As I said, Prohibition was still in effect and a law in the United States. Via the grapevine, we always managed to get a little of the "bubbly" or the hard liquor. In an emergency we always managed to come up with "bathtub gin."

Coming through Customs at Niagara returning to the United States, our gals were very obliging. In expert fashion they were able to secrete several pints each on their person, in such a way as not to destroy their svelte appearance, for the examiners knew that we were a dance troupe.

Our show company, or troupe, call it what you will, at this time having worked closely for almost a year, considered ourselves one big family. Whether star or underling, each was dependent on the other. After playing Minneapolis and St. Paul, bad news surfaced. Our stage manager revealed that our show was being canceled and that we should be prepared to head back to New York in a day or two. Those with previous show business experience always anticipated this type of news, for show business is an unpredictable one.

Arriving back in New York lacked the excitement that was displayed when we were headed for our first show in Boston. Our dance group, being together over a year, developed into a tightly knit group. This was a natural, for we were always rehearsing and sharing new steps with our partners. Aside from working together, we were now all good friends. Each in turn promised, if they received any info regarding a dance call, they would spread the news for the opportunity to be present to audition.

I kept contact with Jimmy Lee, the one who struck his head on a sink at the time of the train accident and Dick, the stand-in for Richard Dix. We thought at this time that we would be able to make up an interesting dance trio. But being in the middle of the summer season, put a dent in show business opportunities.

The three of us practiced together for a short period of time, but auditions and opportunities were nil. Jimmy pulled up stakes and called it quits. He headed for his hometown somewhere in the sunny South. Dick and I kept our ambitions high. He had several years of experience and we worked hard thinking that we had a good comedy dance act.

After Jimmy left, through the grapevine, we learned that a very talented gal named Peggy Lee was available. Chaperoned by her mother made no difference, for her talents were more important, to enhance the act.

Certain movie theaters had vaudeville acts perform on certain nights, mainly weekends, called showing dates. We were booked to play the Superior Theater on

Third Avenue in the vicinity of Thirty-First Street, and we did a one-night stand. We also played another one-night stand at Minsky's Burlesque on Irving Place and Fourteenth Street. Both performances went well and we were greeted with a good applause.

Being realistic, there were no good prospects to look forward to. The future appeared more than dim, and our dreams seemed to have died on the vine. As a result, Dick decided to pull out and go solo. The gal and her mom picked up where they left off. I threw in the towel. It all was a wonderful experience, and I headed for my home once again unemployed. My dad did not have much to say, except that his predictions prevailed.

Nonetheless my family was happy to have me home, after a lengthy absence. Hugs and kisses were the order of the day from my three sisters who seemed to have taken on more beautiful characteristics during my absence. Some conversation took place, and shortly thereafter I retired to my room.

8
Arthur Murray Dance Studios

Meditating alone gave me the opportunity to review all of the experiences thus far in my life. While I felt satisfied that I had given each one of my dreams an honest try, I realized that a more serious approach had to be taken to provide for a more successful future.

My next priority was to contact my dear friend John King. I heard from him on occasion via mail, for he was knowledgeable as to my locations while playing the circuit. We both were ambitious chaps loaded with dreams, but he was more than one step ahead of me, for his goal in life was the legal profession.

I managed to reach him by phone. He was happy to hear that I was home, but the reasons that were responsible for it did not set too well with him. Times Square was our usual meeting location, so a date and time was set. Having met, we resorted to the Automat on Forty-Second Street, where we could select a corner, sipping a cup of coffee with no time limits, and carry ourselves away in conversation. We touched many bases in our lengthy conversation.

I learned that he was scheduled to graduate at the end of this semester. In addition, he stated that he was working part-time at night, from six to ten P.M., as a dance instructor at the Arthur Murray Dance Studio on

Forty-Third Street off Madison Avenue. Upon graduation, he stated that he was offered an opportunity to work for the Dumont Broadcasting Company, in their legal department. I congratulated him. Deep in conversation, it was near midnight and we both decided to head for home. Arrangements were made for another session.

En route home many thoughts ran through my mind. John knew that I had a problem that left me feeling on the sour side.

Even though John was working nights, we had another opportunity for a get-together and we met at our usual location, Times Square about ten-thirty P.M.

John informed me that Arthur Murray was in search of new teachers, both male and female, and was about to start a new training session shortly. He thought that it would be a wonderful opportunity, to give it a try. He indicated that he was doing financially well and without blowing his own horn, he had a good reputation at the studio. I gave in-depth consideration as to what John had told me about a new training class about to start. Considering my recent experience in show business, with knowledge of the waltz and tango, including tap dancing, I decided to apply, for I had nothing to lose, since I was unemployed.

I was interviewed. Upon learning of my background, I guess I was thought to be a good candidate, especially since I had tap dancing to offer, which I understood was not part of their services. Then too, I learned that regardless of what skills one may have had in dancing, they were discounted, and you joined a class of instruction.

There were some forty applicants, both male and female, in the class. Much emphasis was placed on the Arthur Murray method of teaching. The class started as a five-day session, Monday through Friday, from nine A.M.

to five P.M. The program was scheduled for a full month. There was no salary, except for the instructors, who did the teaching. I must comment that they did an excellent job. While these sessions were in progress, observers were present to evaluate the individuals in the class to see if they could meet all standards of the studio. After a month of training, a time was set for a display of each student's ability to handle the teaching process under the watchful eye of Mr. Murray and his staff.

Considering there were forty in the class, only one dozen passed muster. I was fortunate to be one of the twelve.

From my personal observation during this training session, I concluded that if one could walk and feel the beat and rhythm of music, one could learn to dance.

There are only two steps, a walking step, forward or backward, and a sashay, a side step, taken either to the right or left. The combination of these two steps make up the elements for dancing. However, there are other considerations that must be noted. These movements must take place to the rhythm of the music. A one, two, three tempo is a waltz. A one, two, three, four, is for a fox trot. A one, two, three, with a pause on the fourth beat, would be for a tango. The Rhumba and Cha Cha were and are in a class by themselves.

The basic element taught was that one must learn to dance alone on the theory, if one could dance alone, one could lead a partner. Using the same theory, one then could be easily led.

Special emphasis was made for the one being led. This partner must not take a strangle on the leading partner's right arm. If so, it will restrict his movements to lead. The results would not be a graceful picture. The main studio was on Forty-Third Street between Madison and Vanderbilt Avenues. The sections for teaching were luxurious. Drapes were drawn to lean toward privacy. A music box, not a juke box, was in the corner of each studio, where various selections of music could be had by the press of a button, to meet the needs for the lesson.

Another studio, called The Betty Lee or The Betty Ann, was located on the south side of Forty-Fourth Street directly opposite the Murray Studio on the north side of Forty-Third Street. Via a building archway, access could be had to either studio.

To account for the two studios, I learned that some prospective students, who did not favor Mr. Murray, would be assigned to the studio on Forty-Fourth Street, yet would be taught by Murray's staff.

Prospective students, male and female, would be interviewed by select longtime employees of this studio. Each applying student would, at time of interview, via observation, be evaluated from head to foot. Taken into consideration was the manner of dress, hairdos, shoes, nails, perfume, ties, in general, the complete make-up of each individual applying. This evaluation gave the interviewer an idea as to the length of course he would propose. Costs, as I remember, were standard. A six-hour course or a twelve-hour course was usually suggested at five dollars per hour.

Keep in mind, if one's ambition was to learn how to dance, this was the school. However, to be successful, the student had to cooperate. The big hitch was when telling the student that he or she must learn how to dance alone. To some students, to dance alone was no incentive. To offset this situation for starters, the teacher, instead of holding the pupil in an embrace, would place both his hands on the shoulders and go through the teaching movements. This broke the ice with the student, and after a short period, the student was moving about in the arms of the instructor, to the type of music selected.

Dancing is a relaxing exercise. When the art is perfected, it becomes a picture of graceful movements. The bottom line is, the picture created by the movements of two accomplished dancers whirling to the strains of the Strauss "Blue Danube," was comparable to the rhythm and graceful groundswell movements of a smoothly rolling sea.

In one of my experiences, since I had a knowledge of tap dancing, I was given such an assignment to take place at the private home of one of the Morgans, in the vicinity of Thirty-Seventh Street off Madison Avenue. I knew the area well. A library and a museum that covered a square block in the vicinity, were under constant surveillance by private guards.

Approaching the home, I made certain that my appearance was trim. Following formalities, I gained entrance and after introducing myself, was greeted by the mother of the two girls. The youngsters involved were in the twelve-to-fifteen-year bracket. We had an enjoyable session, and the children caught on quickly. The hour passed much too fast. The mother, while evaluating me all the time, was pleased as to how her daughters responded. While only basics can be taught in an hour, I explained to the mother that practice is a necessary element, if one really wanted to accomplish this art. With a thank you, I left to report back to the studio.

Even after a six-hour course, if a student applied him or herself, each could become a fairly good dancer, for they were taught the essentials. Some students caught on quickly to the extent of surprising themselves.

A sort of social gathering was held each Saturday evening. All students were welcome, for it gave them the opportunity to dance with many partners, newcomers as well as longtime experienced dancers. After all, the objective in taking dance lessons was to gain confidence in feeling comfortable with different partners.

Within a short time, my schedule was filled with new students. This in itself was an interesting study in different personalities. There were school girls, working girls, from many fields displaying different levels of education. Then there were the mature women along with the debutantes from Park Avenue, all aspiring to be the belle of the ball. This is what made the job interesting. On the other side of the coin, several mature women, with a good knowledge of dancing, just wanted to be embraced and danced with, for the entire session. In a situation such as this, one had to be alert to and in a professional diplomatic way approach and stress certain basics for better performance. Many personal invitations were received from debutantes to be present at their coming-out parties, so they may stand out among their friends on the dance floor. Studio rules did not approve of these types of invitations; hence this was a no-no! If conduct such as this was disclosed, it meant dismissal for the teacher.

One of my pupils, a widow, senior to me, well preserved, whose husband I learned from conversation was of the medical profession, asked if I would consider visiting her home on Fifth Avenue, for she was planning a social and would appreciate my dancing with her to show her friends how well she was progressing. I thought for a moment and in spite of company rules, that indicated such conduct meant dismissal, I agreed to comply with her wishes. She set the time and date.

I arrived at her home, a fashionable location on Fifth Avenue at the appointed time and hour. Following the procedures for security, I gained entrance, announcing who I was. I was greeted by what I assume was her maid. Many thoughts ran through my mind, for dead silence prevailed with no overtones of any party or gathering in progress.

The maid escorted me to greet my hostess. After a warm handshake, the maid was excused for the evening and I found myself alone with my dancing pupil in a rather more than luxurious apartment. There was no explanation on her part to explain away the absence of any so-called friends or any type of party.

She immediately escorted me on a "Cook's Tour," showing me the beauty of her home. The last room that we entered was her boudoir. She insisted that I enjoy the romantic view from her window overlooking Central park. It was quite a view from our observation point.

The glow of early evening lights reflecting off the park's greenery framed an artistic picture.

We returned to her social study room where I was offered a rather comfortable lounge seat. She took her position opposite me. All this time we engaged in bits of conversation that leaned toward being awkward. Comfortably seated, we engaged in a more fluid type of conversation, covering many fields. She attempted to learn of my future ambitions and goals, a situation that I diplomatically covered, giving no specifics. She had me know that she had young friends in California and how to some extent she was helpful or responsible for them being there.

In all, I spent an hour and a half in general conversation with her. No drinks were offered, not even a glass of water, and most of all, no dancing took place.

When the time seemed appropriate, I suggested leaving, for I had a prior commitment to meet my friend John. She escorted me to the door, and I thanked her for her invite. This was the last time that I ever saw her, even for a dancing session at the studio.

I met John at our usual meeting place, Times Square. We headed for our usual rendezvous, the Automat on Forty-Second Street. My conversation immediately related to my experience that I just had. I explained that I had agreed to dance with a rather special pupil at her apartment, a Fifth Avenue location. I explained how she was supposed to be hosting a special social function, and she wanted her friends to see how well she was progressing with her dancing sessions. The punch line was that there was no party, and no dancing.

John listened carefully and chuckled after I finished my story. He admitted that he has had several such experiences, which at the time seemed awkward and embarrassing, but he had diplomatically worked his way out of each situation.

Imagine what you will, based on her conversation, I was not about to be her paramour or gigolo. After a few coffees in the corner of the automat, where no time limits existed, we called it a night and headed for home.

I dismissed this experience from my mind, even though I had broken company rules. The opportunity did not present itself where she was assigned to me for another studio session, yet my teaching program and assignments continued. To be honest it was a pleasant and an enjoyable job. While I had many wonderful students, none of them have ever become social friends.

Many times, I took stock of myself and gave in-depth thought as to what I was doing for a living. It did not add up. While the job was pleasant, there was no future, yet at the moment it was a source of income. I continued, but I had other plans in my mind for my future.

In retrospect, I, like all young folks, had many

dreams and fantasies. I was trying to find my way in life, as the saying goes today. I satisfied my ego, but I had nothing to show for it. However, I will not discount the many and varied experiences that gave me a better evaluation and perspective of life. The veneer of my dreams had worn off. My fantasies were tarnished. I did what I wanted to do and realized that I was just spinning my wheels and punching the wind. I now was up a cul-de-sac.

9

Delehanty Institute, 1932

Shortly thereafter, I tendered my resignation. Although it came as a surprise, I was thanked for my contribution to the dancing profession.

On January 11, 1932, I enrolled at the Delehanty Institute at 115 East 15th Street in Manhattan. Following some of my dad's advice, considering the benefits of a Civil Service career, I set my sights on a police career. For private reasons the Fire Department did not appeal to me, yet my dad was a Fire Lieutenant at the time. The institute was a well-established school of learning that covered instruction for all courses for positions that required passing a Civil Service examination. Upon enrollment, I was given a complete portfolio of study material, embracing all aspects related to police work. Being presented with all of this material, I realized that I had selected a chore for myself. Working on the premise that nothing comes easy, something that I had already experienced in life, I welcomed this opportunity for opening my life to a new world and career. Physical education, as I was given to understand, was equivalent to fifty percent of the examination. Classes were so arranged that regardless of how an applicant worked, a full program of instruction could always be had.

Realizing that I had enrolled at a Civil Service school

with no job, generated thoughts of me, trying my hand, at getting my old job back at the Public National Bank and Trust Company. If this miracle could happen, it being a night job, would fit well with my daytime schooling.

I remembered a Mr. Dan O'Meara of the Personnel Department and thought, if he were still there, I may get to see him, hoping that he would remember me. My absence now from this bank was a little more than two years, when I left for my professional dancing job in show business. I made several visits to the bank's main office at 76 William Street.

To my surprise, he was still there but had moved up to the rank of Vice President. Working on the premise of "what can I lose," I finally got the opportunity to meet him in his office. To my great surprise, he remembered me. I congratulated him, and we enjoyed a good friendly visit. He asked about my experiences and whether I was still in my new sought position. I opened my heart to him and explained how my short-lived career had ended. I made no plea for getting my old job back, but he could read between the lines and reminded me, since the economy was so poor, the bank was trying hard to keep expenses down. Finishing with a warm feeling and a hand shake, I left.

During the year that seemed to be passing swiftly, I made good use of my daytime hours attending school. The subjects all related to police work, embraced criminal law and procedure, while new to me, proved most interesting. I enjoyed this, for I knew that it would all lead up to an examination for a lifelong career. The physical training I welcomed, for through the years, I had my personal program for private workouts. The class instructors were a breed all their own, having a Fordham College background.

In addition I made at least three visits to my bank

friend, Mr. O'Meara. In August 1933, on my third visit, he surprised me and said that he had an opening for me in the Rack Department. I felt as though a miracle had taken place and before I left, I thanked him profusely.

I was so pleased with myself, especially that my persistent attitude did not result in any annoyance. Working again at night and attending classes three times per week during the day, all fit nicely into my program and seemed to be tailor-made to meet my needs. For certain I knew that the pressure at home would now be lessened, since I would be working again and be able to pursue my new goal in life.

My appearance at the bank at six P.M., on my first night of return, brought several surprised looks from my former co-workers. Handshakes were abundant as well as the many questions asked. Gerald Klein, my former boss, was still in charge. As regards the others, there seemed to have been no changes, for I remembered all the faces.

It was a pleasure to know that I was back working and familiar with the type of work and what would be expected of me. My mind was working overtime, for aside from the pleasure that I had knowing that I was employed again, I wondered what advancement potentials existed at this level. The same five lawyers were still there as well as a gent whom I knew who was holding down this position for some ten years. Dismissing negative thoughts from my mind, I envisioned a full program of working and schooling.

The work schedule was the same, six P.M. to two A.M., six days per week. The heavy periods of the month, the tenth to the fifteenth, were the same. I now made certain that I would get my proper rest. Several social activities had to be rescheduled.

All went well during my first week back. It all seemed like "old hat," sorting checks, recording and tallying to match those of the branches' accounts.

I attended my scheduled classes with new energies, for this was to be my goal in life, God willing.

Fiorella LaGuardia was Mayor at this time. The economy was definitely downhill, the aftermath of the Depression years. All city departments were feeling the economic pinch. Civil Service was dormant in the area of holding examinations. As it was, no appointments had been made to the Police Department for several years. As a matter of fact, I don't believe that an eligible list of candidates existed at this time.

My program was well started, alternating working at night and attending school three times per week. The study field was so broad that research, review, and home study seemed endless. After months of study, I met new friends, classmates all with the same ambitions.

Every so often so-called trial exams were held, patterned after past official exams. The school published lists of those who took the exam. This gave the opportunity to make comparisons as to where one placed versus his friends.

Memory tests played an important part. One would have the opportunity to examine a detailed picture for about ten minutes and then be questioned about its contents. For example: What time was it? The car registration? The state of issue? The type of weather, since umbrellas were carried, etc.

True and false exams were nonexistent at this time. These types of examinations were resorted to at a later date for expediency to obtain a list of successful candidates.

Months went by quickly. The study material became

more in-depth. There was no rumor as to what the Civil Service Commission was planning. As a result the course given for patrolman, was extended, to include the material that was embraced in the Sergeants, the Lieutenants, and Captains home study. This move by the school created a deeper interest in the students, resulting in the student having a greater knowledge of what was required in police work.

In addition to all the lectures and study material, students became involved in a strenuous physical training program. The instructors were the epitome of physical fitness, a condition each student hoped to attain.

An interesting note, one of the instructors named Al Reach, at one time was a contender in the heavyweight division of boxing. He contributed his skills and talents to self-defense, boxing and wrestling.

Attending to my responsibilities at the bank, together with attending school and home study, the months just rolled by. Without draining my energies, I minimized my social activities. Then too, my responsibilities at home were lessened.

Attending classes now for a rather long period of time, afforded the opportunity to acquire many new friends. This gave the occasion for many personal sessions after class about the subject matter given. It was most interesting to listen to another's evaluation of what was lectured upon.

Opportunities in the business sector were still nil. This was responsible for the huge number of applicants who registered for this position. Fortunately, I was working, hence, I experienced very little pressure and concentrated heavily on my schoolwork.

It did not take too long for the bank officials to realize that the Depression was being reflected in the daily transactions of their various branches. Volume dropped considerably. One could sense that the bank officials were about to take some positive corrective action. These thoughts gave me an insecure feeling, for I only recently had been rehired.

My boss, Mr. Klein, realized this, at his level, for he and his staff were the so-called nerve pulse of all of its branch activities. Some nights we were ready to leave by twelve midnight. In the light of good judgment, he would arrange the tempo of work received, so his forces worked at least to two A.M. each night.

We learned that efficiency experts would be paying us a visit in the Rack Department. This they did. All could envision a weeding-out procedure, but how? Those who represented the efficiency group, on appearance introduced themselves. They explained what and why all this was happening.

Each of the staff was given a batch of checks, weighing in the area of one pound, for the purpose of processing, sorting, tallying, etc., on the Burroughs machine. The efficiency man stood by with a stopwatch in his hand. When each individual's chore was finished, it was checked for accuracy. The results were obvious for some of the staff lost out. Fortunately, I passed the test and was retained.

On the other side of the coin, school sessions were becoming more interesting, particularly since I was able to hold my job. At no time did I reveal to my co-workers my aim in life, especially since what had happened.

Shortly thereafter, as though a miracle had taken place, the economic situation started to spurt. It became noticeable in each day's receipts. I am happy to know that the bank officials recognized this almost sudden change. I understand that those who were let go had the opportunity to return if they so desired. This took place and the family of the Rack Department workers were together again.

Work and my classes were well coordinated. Yes, there was stress and strain, for I was always on the go. The trial examinations were held periodically. When the results were published, I was satisfied that I was absorbing and retaining all of the materials. My newly acquired school friends became more meaningful. The rigid routine of gym work started to show benefits.

Patience is virtue. After months of dedication to both work and school, a rumor from school spread that the Civil Service Commission was planning to hold a police examination in 1934. Since no date was set, it was like dropping one shoe. If this information were true, I set my mind at full throttle, ready to sprint to a successful finish.

When a date was set to file and the applications were available, the revolving doors at the Municipal Building got a workout. How well I remember that day. Appearing early, I joined with crowds, forcing my way into the building.

An examination date was set, which meant that the medical and physical examinations were to be held first. Of the 24,000 applicants who filed, 12,000 did not pass the medical and physical examination. This meant that they were automatically eliminated from taking the written examination. However, those who failed had the opportunity to file for an appeal.

Since 12,000 were eligible for the written examination, Civil Service decided to hold ten different examinations, all relevant to police work. It was stressed that no two examinations would be alike. The order in which one filed would determine what numbered examination would be taken, a sort of first-come, first-served situation. I, being one of the group to file first, was notified that I would be taking examination number one.

On the day set, I arrived early. The location was Grand Central Palace in Manhattan. I experienced a lot of tense moments. I was determined that I had to be successful, for this was my goal in life. I purposely avoided talking to and avoiding my friends, so as not to disturb my trend of thoughts. I felt like a race horse in the starting gate.

Several monitors were already in the room that I was directed to. In a short period, the room was full, but each applicant was equally spaced from his neighbor. One of the monitors, I assume in-charge, introduced himself and made a few remarks regarding conduct during the examination. The papers were distributed. Upon hearing the signal to start, I made a quick survey of what was handed me.

I monitored my time piece to make certain that I gave only the proper time in writing my answer to each question. The memory and the mathematics part of the test were given as separate entities. A partial dead silence now existed for a good three-hour period. When the finish bell sounded and all the paperwork was collected, sighs of relief could be heard. On leaving, those friends whom I purposely avoided gave nods of recognition and in a group we left the building, holding a session on the sidewalk. A few comments were made as to how I answered this or that question, but conversation was limited. To take the sting out of what we just experienced, we resorted to the nearest pub to down a few to take the edge off of our feelings.

On the way home, I tried to remember certain questions that at the time posed a problem and the efforts that I made to record the correct answers. The pressure that I experienced to some extent still existed and it took awhile for me to unwind. Arriving home, my family wanted to know how I made out? I explained the confidence that I had in answering all questions and let it go at that.

When all ten official examinations had been completed, and the exam date became past history, the Delehanty School gave the opportunity for many sessions to review all ten examinations. The students made it their priority to attend at least one of these scheduled sessions, especially the one that covered the examination that they had taken. Having attended the session that dealt with examination number one, the one that I had taken, I made certain to listen intently and take notes. At home with vivid indelible impressions on my mind as to answers I submitted, I made a mental comparison with those suggested by the school. With fingers crossed and not displaying any overconfidence, I was satisfied with how I handled the matter. Meeting many friends at the session I attended resulted in a great deal of further chit-chat on the subject matter.

It took several days for me to settle down, for now I only had to attend to my nightly job. The pressures that I had felt for some time were now easing off. The next on the agenda was a waiting game, until the official results of the examination were promulgated.

At work I did not make any disclosures of my intentions, especially the fact that I had recently taken the police examination. As a result each night on the job was the same as the night before, and the night that would follow.

Anxiety in a situation such as I was experiencing could have become overbearing. As a result, I had to shelve my thoughts and as I said before, a waiting game now existed.

The days and weeks passed quickly. Months followed

in like fashion. While some of the employees at the bank, some time back, were released via the efficiency project, were again rehired, but the economy was still iffy. Nonetheless I was drawing a pay check, twenty-five dollars per a six-day work week, for the banks were still open a half-day on Saturdays. While the salary was not considered a windfall, it was a good one, which helped pay the bills.

Not having to attend lecture classes anymore, prompted me to stay with the physical education program, for good workouts always appealed to me. Al Reach, the former heavyweight boxing contender, was still there, which seemed to be a drawing card in itself. Then too, being so close to school, there was always the possibility of hearing some kind of rumor regarding the results or at least the possible date when the official results would be published.

A rather lengthy period of time had elapsed, when the *Civil Service Leader,* a popular much-read newspaper by City and State employees, finally published the results of the ten examinations taken in 1934. The official list was then promulgated on July 17, 1935. The Delehanty Institute, my alma mater, was flooded with telephone calls and visits from candidates inquiring as to their position on the official list, since they had a copy.

Before I had the opportunity to scan the list, I bought the paper and read that I placed number 233 on the list. When I arrived home, a Civil Service letter waiting for me confirmed the information, with a document stating that I passed and my official position was 233 on the list. My family was delighted, particularly my dad. With the position that I was on the list, it was considered "in the money," meaning that I was certain of appointment at some future date. In retrospect of the 24,000 applicants who had filed, 12,000 failed the medical and physical exam. There were 5,504 on the list just promulgated. The ratings were so close that the final averages were rated to at least four decimal points.

I found it hard to contain my feelings, yet I made no disclosure among my coworkers at the bank. I made an attempt to put all my experiences behind me, for now I was assured of my definite goal in life. As a result my anxieties had subdued, and I continued my bank position as though nothing had happened.

As I indicated before, nothing new happened at work, except for the period from the 10th to the 15th of each month when the work became heavy, then we started at three P.M., instead of six P.M.

I could feel the personal difference as a result of being free from all the prior stress and pressures. Some nights when we finished work in the area of one A.M., we, not all, decided to bowl a few games at 15 Park Row, an alley that was open all night. If I remember correctly, it was twenty-five cents per game and the alleys had no automatic pin set-up facilities. Nonetheless we played a few games before we left for home. On Saturday nights into Sunday morning, some of us attended the two A.M. printers Mass at St. Andrew's Catholic Church on Duane Street in the area of the Municipal Building and City Hall.

To alternate, at least three times per week, I would attend the physical sessions that I enrolled in at the school. My activities, being spaced properly, all made for an enjoyable program, which I could handle easily without stress.

Mayor Fiorello LaGuardia was still at the helm and the City was working with a lean budget. Unemployment figures ran an all-time high with a 12 million figure, including professional as well as non-skilled workers.

There was a dire need for more police since none had been appointed for some five years, mainly because of the City's financial condition and there being no list. Someone gave birth to the idea of conducting a Police Pre-service Training Course. Apparently all the City Fathers approved and the plan was set in motion. The first one thousand men on the list were solicited to find out how well this plan would be received. Thinking for all that were solicited, I deeply felt that if someone opposed the offer, when official time for appointment came, they would or could be passed over. The reason being, for at this time Civil Service could select one candidate out of every three. I would imagine that the response was favorable if not 100 percent.

Notices from the City were received, outlining the program, indicating that it would be a flexible one to meet everyone's needs and or desires. Governor's Island, a military base in New York Harbor, was the stage set for military drill, alternating with an armory in the Bronx for study and instruction.

It was clearly understood, with the signing of papers, that the time spent in this program would not be counted or considered as time spent in the department. In addition papers were signed absolving the City of any responsibility and liability, if one should sustain any injury.

Receiving this opportunity shed a new light that required the adjustment of my daily and weekly programs. Personally, I was pleased with the project, for it seemed now, that each day spent would be nearer to the day of my official appointment.

From my viewpoint, without doubt it was a terrific yet demanding project. The military drill and training were similar to army regulations. My daily programs, now consisted in ferrying to Governor's Island; then via subway to the Bronx Armory and then back to Manhattan to William and Liberty Streets, the location of the bank. To envision all this seemed hectic, but I managed it all real well.

Again days and weeks passed by quickly, and my schedule now seemed routine. I assume that this pre-service program was doing well, for whatever session I attended either at the island or the armory, was always a full house.

I saw many of my old schoolmates, those whom I got to know through the years, while attending classes. Traveling from one location to the other, our thoughts were pooled. All seemed to feel that if this opportunity was not accepted it may prove fatal, for in the final analysis, one could be passed over, since Civil Service could pick only one out of every three on the list, when the official time for induction took place.

Getting used to this intensive program took some time. I, working still at night, had to make several changes in my schedules, so as to be able to handle both jobs.

When there is definite goal and purpose in mind, you make sure that you cover all bases. Some nine months went by, attending religiously, all sessions of drilling and study in this Pre-Service Training Course.

An official notice was received one day that the City would induct the first 250 names on the list for official assignment to the New York City Police Academy. My position on the list was 233, so I knew that I was included in this group.

I still made no revelations to my co-workers at the bank. I may have felt a little skeptical, for I wanted to be certain, at least, that my ambitions were coming to fruition.

Then word was received that the official appointments would be made on March 9, 1936. I continued working at the bank each night as though nothing unusual was happening. But inwardly I had a potpourri of feelings that if analyzed would spell out all emotions. As yet I had received no official notice.

Through official channels on March 9, 1936, I received a notice from Civil Service, stating that the 250 investigations had not been completed, that the date for my induction would be March 19, 1936. This one notice hit two bull's eye targets, for March 19, 1936 was and is the feast day of St. Joseph, my patron Saint, hence it had a double meaning for me.

This pre-service training course had already been discontinued on receipt of the first official notice. All the candidates felt that things were beginning to take shape now. My next problem was how and when I could get to my friend, the Vice President, Mr. O'Meara, at the bank, to tell him that I would be leaving and why. Then too, I had an obligation to say good-bye to my co-workers after a close relationship after so many years.

The opportunity presented itself, and I found myself in Mr. O'Meara's office. If I were a family member, I could not have received a more warm welcome. He asked how I was making out and that he was happy to learn that I survived the efficiency test, at the time when things were running a little rough and the bank was cutting some of its staff.

After exploring and friendly conversation, the ball being in my court, I finally explained the reason for my visit. Looking him straight in the eyes, I said that I was informing him of my resignation. He, looking a little puzzled, asked why?

I revealed my ambitions, that after all these years, I thought that I would try my hand in an attempt to join the New York City Police Force. He gave me the opportunity to work nights. As a result I took the opportunity to go to school in the daytime to prepare and study for several years in preparation. I explained how recently I had taken and passed the examination, placing number 233 on the list and scheduled for appointment on March 19, 1936. He jumped up from behind his desk, I, not knowing what to expect, he shook my hand to congratulate me. He then said, "I am glad to see someone with enough sense to leave, for there are no opportunities here." He shook my hand again and wished me well.

His attitude was so warm and encouraging that upon leaving his office, I felt more like family than a resigning employee. My next priority was to bid adieu to my co-workers with whom I enjoyed working through the years. They were all good, hard-working family men. Handshakes were many and well wishes were abundant. I promised that if I were assigned to a local precinct, I would pay them a visit some night in full regalia.

Completing my obligations at work, it felt as though the curtain had fallen, closing a final chapter in my life. Reminiscing on my early years, abundant with many dreams and ambitions, I experienced all these fantasies to no avail. I was ready to embrace a new lasting career facing unknown challenges.

Within a few days, I received a letter from the bank, congratulating me and wishing me success. Enclosed was a severance pay check for two weeks' salary.

Standing tall and much impressed by my overcoming many challenges, I was prepared to attend and assume the responsibilities of my new position in life, that of a New York City police officer to be sworn in on March 19, 1936.

I was assigned to the Police Academy for a two-month period. After graduation exercises that took place in City Hall Park, off Park Row in Manhattan, I was assigned to patrol duty in the Seventh Precinct in Manhattan.

Remarks

The names in the book are not fictitious.

The author did not touch on any of the intimate relationships with his family. These were and are private matters. Our family was a closely knit group.

My mom was a gentle, loving, and understanding soul, as all mothers should be. My dad was a good provider but was a bit short on warmth for his offspring. He lacked flexibility, to the extent that he thought all his children should share the same traits and personalities.

At age twelve, a time he often referred to, he did a man's job to help support his family. Hence, he had no childhood, one of the most precious times of our existence. Therefore, I have on several occasions referred to him as a "tough taskmaster." Having visited him many times in the fire house, he appeared to have a different personality there with the men whom he supervised. Listening to stories related to him by his co-workers, if they were little offbeat, he tried to equate them to his children, a situation that seemed unfair.

My sisters all grew to be lovely young ladies. Having a great responsibility in caring for them in early years, resulted in my closeness to them through the years.

When I left the nest, I took my marriage vows twice at Our Lady Chapel in St. Patrick's Cathedral on Fifth Avenue in Manhattan.

When I changed course in my life's goal and left the

Prep Seminary, I knew that it was to some degree a shock to both my parents. I was told that had I continued, my family upon ordination would have presented me with a Chalice as a lasting memory. Instead, on becoming a New York City police officer, I was presented with a .38-caliber revolver, the tool of my profession, plus prayers for my protection.